Chicken Soup for the Soul.

Every Day's a Gift

Amy Newmark

CSS

Chicken Soup for the Soul, LLC
Cos Cob, CT

Chicken Soup for the Soul: Every Day's a Gift
Amy Newmark

Published by Chicken Soup for the Soul, LLC www.chickensoup.com
Copyright © 2019 by Chicken Soup for the Soul, LLC.

The publisher gratefully acknowledges the many publishers and individuals who granted Chicken Soup for the Soul permission to reprint the cited material.

Front cover photo courtesy of Stockphoto.com/Irochka_T (© Irina Tischenko).
Photo of Amy Newmark courtesy of Susan Morrow at SwickPix

Cover and Interior by Daniel Zaccari

ISBN: 978-1-61159-705-9

PRINTED IN THE UNITED STATES OF AMERICA
on acid∞free paper

25 24 23 22 21   02 03 04 05 06 07 08 09 10 11

Table of Contents

Every Day a Friday

*Monday is a lame way to spend
1/7 of your life.
~Author Unknown*

I love Fridays, and I'm not alone. Most people associate the last day of the workweek with feelings of relief, relaxation, and anticipation of good times to come in the weekend ahead. You know there has to be something special about a day when the feeling of celebration that accompanies its arrival is even commemorated in the name of a restaurant chain!

And so I, too, celebrate Fridays. After dropping

my son off at school I head to Starbucks, to pick up a coffee treat of one type or another. Then instead of driving straight home I generally take a long route through the most scenic roads I can find, which usually includes my favorite corner of the local state park. On and on throughout the day I find myself smiling and happy for no other reason than that the day's name starts *with an "F" rather than a "M," "T," or "W."*

When I pick my son up again hours into the afternoon we high-five physically and vocally, our chorus of "FRIDAY!" resonating at least as loudly as our hand slap. Then we point out to each other the signs of beginning celebration in the college town we drive through. We see footballs being passed on fraternity lawns, hamburgers being thrown on grills, people parked on front porch swings, and parties everywhere swinging into action. Sometimes it seems as if the whole world is celebrating Friday!

The other day I emerged from a doctor's office happy over a positive prognosis in a health situation

I was concerned about. My good mood was amplified by the signs of spring that were bursting all around me—flowers blossoming, birds singing, bright sunshine warm upon my back. I was suddenly ready to celebrate, and java-scented thoughts wafted through my brain. I whispered the word "Cappuccino!" and headed for the specialty coffee bar that was conveniently located just around the corner.

My mind rebelled. "What are you doing? It's Tuesday! Coffee treats are reserved for Fridays!" And suddenly I realized how ridiculous that line of thinking was! Why should Fridays be any more special than any other day of the week? Why waste six days while waiting to rejoice on the seventh? Minutes later I was walking back to my car with a big grin on my face and a raspberry mocha in my hand.

A small victory, to be sure, but it's also an accurate example of how many of us live our lives. We're waiting for conditions to be right before we allow ourselves to enjoy our time here on earth. Maybe when we finally graduate from college and get a job it will be time to celebrate, or perhaps when our toddlers are old enough to be in school all day. We'll rejoice when the car is paid off, or enjoy life when we're finally able to retire. And in that waiting we waste so much of the life that God has given us and the happiness that can be found in our todays. What if we moved a little of that "Friday feeling" into our rainy-day Mondays, our gloomy Tuesdays and our mid-week Wednesdays? Surely our lives would be much happier as a result.

It's interesting to note that T.G.I. Friday's isn't open for business on just the last day of the work-week! No, they celebrate all week long and into the weekend.

So should we.

—Elaine L. Bridge—

The Gift of Brain Cancer

The excursion is the same when you go
looking for your sorrow as when you go
looking for your joy.
~Eudora Welty

In August 2002, I received the greatest gift of my life when I was told that I had terminal brain cancer and would be dead in four to six months. I had been married exactly five months when this happened. My career was going well, my family and friends loved me. I was as happy as I had ever been. So why was this such a great gift? Why?

Because I had to face my death.

It was the middle of the night in January 2003. I was wandering outside in the cold, alone and bitter. The clinical trial I had entered was fraught with uncertainty and danger. I could only participate because I was terminal, my survival quite unlikely. I was confused, constantly nauseous, and hardly able to walk, even with a cane.

I was infuriated by my circumstances: I hated the cancer, myself, the doctors, and God. I found myself shouting, screaming, crying, raging against the injustice. For the first time in fifty-four years I had finally found happiness in my life, and now this horrific disease was ripping from me not only the joy of life, but also any semblance of stability, comfort or peace. Was I destined for continuous detestable rotting away every day in my pathetic limp to a cold grave?

Then suddenly, amidst all the virulence, came the inspirational voice of a very dear old friend, employer, and mentor, W. Clement Stone, one of the first people to write about Positive Mental Attitude, or PMA. In my mind I could hear him say, as he had thousands of times, "Every Adversity carries within it the seed of equivalent or greater benefit to those who have a Positive Mental Attitude!"

What?

Are you serious?

Greater Benefit?

What on earth was the greater benefit of dying of brain cancer, old man? (I was unaware that Mr. Stone had passed away just five months earlier at the age of 100.)

His words kept running through the part of my brain that was still functioning. Not some adversity, he had said, but every adversity, EVERY adversity, carries within it that seed of equivalent or greater benefit! You have to be kidding!

Fortunately, the many years of his being my mentor, teacher and hero had left its mark—the words "I reasoned" were ablaze like sun above my head. He used "I reasoned" frequently—very often in describing critical situations he faced in life. Once, a loaded gun was held to his head by a desperate, depressed, and hopeless person who told him that he had lost everything—he was going to kill Mr. Stone, and then turn the gun on himself. While most of us would panic in such a spot, Mr. Stone said calmly, "I reasoned," and then proceeded to think of a logical plan to save not only himself but the other person as well. He later set the person up in business, where the man was successful and prosperous the rest of his life.

"So," I said to myself, giving in to his message, "Let's reason." Immediately, I was at peace and felt rational—for the first time in months.

So… what were the possibilities for me? After all, life at that point had not provided me with very good options.

I certainly didn't have the option of "live happily ever after"—or did I?

The fact is one of two things was going to happen: I was either going to die very shortly, or, much less likely, live a long time.

So what if I died soon?

Well, "I reasoned," if I were bitter and angry, then I would have spent the last few months of my life in sorrow and isolation, making a living hell for my loved ones, and would be remembered, if at all, as a bitter old man who let brain cancer defeat him. I would receive their temporary show of sympathy, but in the end they would only have contempt for me and how I left them.

On the other hand, what if I were positive and hopeful? It wouldn't change the date of my death one bit!

But, it would mean that I would spend the last months of my life breathing deeply and clearly, contented, blissful, and in love with my family and everyone I met. I would die a happy man, and be remembered as that brave soul who faced a terrible death with courage, fortitude and aplomb. I would be cherished by those who knew me.

On the other hand, what if I made it? What if

I lived?

Then I had no reason to be bitter and tormented! Why waste months of my life wailing about an end that wasn't even near?

So there it was—I had every reason to be positive about my condition, and absolutely no reason to be negative.

It was at that point, that very moment in time, for the first time in my life, that I stopped dying and started living.

I started telling everyone I met and knew that having brain cancer was the greatest thing that had ever happened to me, and today I believe that with all my heart.

A little over a year ago, I learned that the brain cancer had returned. Treatment today is more researched and predictable, prognosis is better; however, the outcome is never certain. After a year of radiation and chemotherapy the tumor board doctors have decided to continue my chemotherapy indefinitely and have scheduled me for monthly MRIs, with absolutely no promises.

How has this disturbing news affected me? It has made me even more positive!

From that special moment—that cold, dark night in January 2003, I have not wasted one second of my life fretting about dying. All the moments of all of my days are spent living.

Brain cancer the first time made me a better man. The second time is making me a good man. Brain cancer is the greatest thing that has ever happened to me.

So what about you? You will have good things and bad in life. Sometimes life will give you great fortune, other times it will rip you like a brick across the face.

What happens to you will happen, and you only have two ways to respond—you can be positive and happy, or negative and miserable. That's it. The good news is that the choice is always up to you! You choose how happy you will be every day of your life, every way that life happens, no matter when, no matter what, no matter who.

Make the decision today to live, not die. To be positive, not negative. Don't endure a tragedy such as mine to figure it out. Live every day, live every minute, live every second of your life.

—Tom Schumm—

It's in the Little Things

*Enjoy the little things, for one day you may
look back and realize they were the big things.*
~Robert Brault, www.robertbrault.com

It was one of those days when there was way too much to do. I had fallen behind in most of my household chores. I hadn't been to the grocery store in nearly forever and we were out of pretty much everything. The laundry was piled up well above the tops of the hampers and the house was stretching even my reasonably loose standards of cleanliness. And besides all that, I had two article deadlines and needed to spend some serious time at my computer.

All of that, and my four children were on a break from school. They were thrilled to be home and asked me repeatedly how we would spend their day off.

They were going to be disappointed with my plans for the day. There was absolutely nothing fun about them. Nothing special, nothing school break-worthy at all.

The kids woke up that morning, expecting their usual bowls of cold cereal. But we were out of milk, and my kids hate dry cereal. There were no eggs and no bread, which left few breakfast options. I searched through the freezer, hoping for a box of frozen waffles. No such luck. I rooted around in the fridge, finally finding a tube of buttermilk biscuits. I sprinkled them with cinnamon and sugar, baked them, and gave them to the kids.

"I'm sorry that I can't offer you anything better this morning, but I haven't had time to go shopping," I said. The kids didn't bother responding. They were too busy shoving my makeshift cinnamon rolls into their mouths.

After breakfast, I started a load of laundry and sat down at the computer. My youngest daughter, Julia, walked toward me, wearing her I'm-about-to-whine face. "But, Mommy, I thought we were going to do something fun today," she said. "Since it's our day off from school."

"I know it's your day off, but it's not Mommy's day off," I explained. "I have work to do."

"Can you play a game with me?" she begged. "Like *Candy Land*? Or beauty shop?"

I sighed. I really didn't have time to play. I desperately needed to get some work done. But then I had an idea. "Can we play beauty shop while I work?"

So I got my article done, and my toenails painted at the same time.

My oldest, Austin, volunteered to fix lunch so I could keep working. The younger kids were thrilled with his selections. Not exactly the choices the food pyramid people advise, but the kids had fun and I met my writing deadlines.

Shortly after lunch, we made the trek to the grocery store. Austin pushed the cart, while the younger kids collected coupons from the little dispensers scattered throughout the store. I got what I needed—with a few additions from my entourage, of course.

Back at home, the kids decided to play "grocery store" with the coupons they had collected during our trip. They lined up the canned goods on the kitchen counters and the snacks on the island and pretended to re-buy our groceries.

For the remainder of the afternoon, I cleaned house, folded laundry, and started dinner. The kids continued with their game until my husband, Eric, walked through the door.

He spotted me and grinned. "So how was the kids' big day off today?"

I began to explain that we hadn't done anything special because I'd been too busy with chores. But the kids interrupted me.

"Daddy, did you see Mommy's toenails? She let me sit under her computer desk and paint them while she typed!" Julia said. "It was so much fun!"

"And, Dad, we had the best breakfast today," said Austin. "Have you ever made those special biscuits for Dad? They were awesome!"

Eric gave me a questioning look and all I could do was shrug. My two middle kids, Jordan and Lea, piped up to tell their dad about the coupon game and Austin's special lunch. "We had such a great day today, Dad! It was a blast!"

I looked at my children's faces. They were lit up with excitement. Excitement about makeshift cinnamon rolls, a most unhealthy lunch, coupons from the grocery store, and painted toenails.

"You guys really had a good day? You're not disappointed that we didn't do something fun?" I asked.

Austin shrugged and said, "Life is only as fun as you make it, Mom."

I nodded, realizing how right he was. Happiness is far more about our attitude than our circumstances.

I hugged my kids and thanked them for reminding me to look for happiness in the little things.

Julia smiled and said, "And the little things that make you the happiest are us, right, Mommy?"

Wow, my kids sure are smart.

—Diane Stark—

In Full Bloom

*Some people are always grumbling because
roses have thorns; I am thankful that
thorns have roses.*
~Alphonse Karr

She was outside, looking at the flowers. "I don't think I mentioned this earlier, but one of my hobbies is taking photos of flowers," she said, contemplating the few blooms left in my yard. "Let me get my camera."

"Knock yourself out," I shrugged, wondering why anyone would bother. I had not planted much this year, cutting back on nearly everything since losing my job. But if she wanted to take pictures...

It had been a difficult year. Just when I thought I was done with the bitterness, it would all come rushing back. The last thing on my mind was flowers.

She aimed her lens at a rose. I hadn't seen her in nearly twenty years, since college in New York. The world had changed, yet we seemed the same. We could still party like old times, as long as we were home by eleven, wore comfortable shoes, and took a couple of aspirin and an antacid. And since we couldn't see our crows' feet without our reading glasses, essentially we were the same. Close enough, I reasoned.

I fiddled with the television remote. My laptop was on the coffee table next to a magazine I was reading. That was me, doing a dozen things at once, packing everything I could into a moment. I was busy with graduate school, an arduous job search, and being the stereotypical valiant, strong, single mother of two boys.

She steadied herself near the last rose of the season, quiet and still, taking photo after photo.

Eventually even the dog got bored with her endeavor and walked away.

Suddenly a song from *Mary Poppins* filled the air. I was pretty sure it was coming from outside my head. This day was getting progressively stranger.

"That's my cell phone," she remarked. "I set the alarm on it to remind me to take my medicine. 'Spoonful of Sugar'—get it?"

"An alarm for meds?" I laughed. "Are we that old?" I still refused to write grocery lists, insisting on carrying the list around in my head. I'd forgotten many things that way, but so what? It was the principle of the thing. I would get old when I was good and ready.

Anger kept me young, I figured. Those days were bittersweet, my fury harsh but healthy.

"Strange looking pills," I remarked as she pulled them from her purse.

"They're for my liver," she took a drink of water. "Actually, it's not MY liver. I'm just borrowing it." One corner of her mouth curled upward.

Every few hours, Anne took anti-rejection medication to keep her body from attacking her donated organ. Eight years earlier, she had been diagnosed with a rare liver disorder, one so rare that her doctor missed it completely. Somehow, though, she knew something was wrong. But she didn't know exactly what.

"It was a fluke, really," she said. "What are the chances of meeting a liver specialist at a party? And he was cute!"

She had a slew of flukes in her life. After her liver transplant, she came down with thyroid cancer, discovered by chance during a checkup by a doctor touching the base of her throat. "I told him he was examining the wrong end of me," she giggled. She could giggle at the damndest things.

One day she felt dizzy. With her track record, her doctor sent her for an MRI, which revealed a small tumor in her brain. "It's no bigger than your fingernail, and it hasn't grown at all, so that's a good sign. After all, size is everything!" That was

Anne—ever hopeful, giggling and fluky. Even a brain tumor was not beyond joking about. I envied her attitude, but certainly not her situation.

She'd be leaving soon. I was just fine alone. It was great to have her here, share old times, but I was comfortable on my own. I didn't need anybody.

With a hug, she was off. I grabbed a beer from the fridge.

Later that day, an e-mail popped up from her, taking forever and a day to load, especially to an impatient, moody grump like me. Sheesh, I huffed, I have things to do.

It was filled with her flower photos—still, clear, and beautiful. She had taken a few blooms and made them glow, made them perfect, made them timeless. Just a few raggedy flowers.

Damn, I thought. She had gotten past the anger, past the pity. She was on the other side, capturing giggles and picking flowers, making an incredible, everlasting bouquet while I grumbled and whined. That, too, wasn't fair.

I wanted to be able to do that. Here I was trying to cram all sorts of events into my life so it would count for something, as she blithely took one moment at a time, polished it until it shined, and shared it with everyone. She made it look easy. Compared to many things in her life, I guess it was.

Quietly she was able to stop the world from turning, keep it still for a moment, insisting that it take the time to look at a single, lowly daisy. Even more extraordinary, the world would do it.

"Wow," I wrote back. "These are incredible." Lame, I know, but for once I was beyond words.

"Annie," she replied, knowing what I was thinking. "We don't know what tomorrow will be. We don't know if we'll even have a tomorrow. So I choose to focus on today. That's why I take pictures. That's why I came to visit you. That's why I'm here."

I shifted my gaze to outside. I got it now. I was stubborn and thickheaded but finally I got it. And I had thought I was the strong one.

She'll be back to visit again—I'm sure of it. Until

then, I have her flowers, in full bloom. Actually, I always had them, but it was Anne who got me to really see them.

—Annie Mannix—

A Timely Lesson

We can only be said to be alive in those moments when our hearts are conscious of our treasures.
~Thornton Wilder

"The kid was only eighteen. He dropped on the basketball court. SADS. It's what a lot of those young athletes die of."

"Yeah, what's SADS?"

"Sudden Arrhythmia Death Syndrome."

As I listened to the actor's words on *NCIS*, I popped up on the couch, dumping *The New York Times* crossword onto the floor. Extricating myself from the heavy paws of our Lab-mix, Yoshi, I moved to the computer and typed in "SADS."

I wove through research about this syndrome, which is characterized by a cardiac electrical glitch. It was probably what had snuffed out our teenaged son's life seventeen years earlier. Maybe if Josh had been born later, he could have been saved. SADS no longer had to result in sudden death, but it was genetic, so close relatives should be examined.

Jeff and I have always been grateful that our third child, Maliq, born eighteen years after our first, has had solid ground under his feet. Life has tossed this kid very few lemons.

Young life was different for our middle child, Miles. Losing his big brother when he was only eight cast a shadow across his childhood. Miles had held hands with mortality too early. Now at twenty-seven, he was a father himself.

I called him to talk about getting checked for SADS.

"Mom, I had an EKG a few months ago because I had those bruised ribs. They didn't find a problem.

Are you worried? Should I be? For Mikah?"

Miles hadn't planned on children. He brought his dad and me the ultrasound picture as a way to tell us that he was going to be a father. He was happy. And terrified.

"Mom, all that can go wrong..."

"Yeah, but all that can go right. Look at you; look at Maliq."

There's a lot Jeff and I, as parents, don't get worked up about since Josh died; fender-benders, money problems, adolescent piercings, and pretty much anything that isn't a death threat stays in perspective.

***

Now we were having Maliq checked for SADS. The doctor and nurse swept into the small exam room that was packed full of our family. The doc took one look at Maliq, who even when seated, dwarfed him, and began firing questions: History of eye problems, scoliosis, heart murmurs? I knew where he was going because I had already been there during one of my many Internet searches. Marfan's Syndrome.

"Listen Doctor, I understand I'm not a cardiologist, but I've researched Marfan's thoroughly. Maliq doesn't fit the criteria." I knew even as the sentences flew anxiously out of my mouth that this doctor wasn't taking me seriously.

"How tall are you, anyway?" Just fifteen, Maliq already measured in at 6'3". The cardiologist put stethoscope to chest. His face changed. He listened for a long time, then had his nurse listen.

Damn, I knew that expression. I had seen it enough times with Josh. I looked over at Jeff. His face seemed to lose muscle, sagged as he too recognized the shift.

The doc listened again. "There's definitely a murmur."

Maliq's face, lean and sculpted, was open and mostly unconcerned.

"I think this young man has Marfan's Syndrome."

Maliq looked at us, then at the doc. "What's that?"

"It's a syndrome that includes serious heart problems. Young man, as of right now, you are on complete athletic restriction."

Maliq's eyes registered shock as tears rolled down his face. Maliq's world was spinning. The door was slamming shut on the life he had constructed, on the future he had assumed. Maliq had been a soccer goalkeeper since he was four.

Miles moved to his brother's side, put his arm around Maliq, moved his head in close and whispered in his ear. Time paused as I watched my sons together. Their relationship deepened in that moment, narrowing the span of years between them.

I jumped in to compensate for the doc's obviously underdeveloped bedside manner, my voice stern enough to cause my husband to grimace, and Miles to smile.

"What other tests are needed to confirm or rule

out the diagnosis, and when can we get them done?"

The cardiologist looked startled by my tone and set of my jaw. Years of navigating the medical system had helped me be just a little scary, when need be.

"We can do the EKG here. He needs to go over to the hospital for the echo cardiogram."

Maliq had rearranged his face, stopped his tears.

They squeezed the machine into the room. Jeff and I sighed in relief when no long QT, which is a marker related to SADS, and no other abnormality showed in the EKG's squiggly lines.

My schedule was such that I would take Maliq over to the U for the echo. As we walked to the car, I reached up to hug Maliq. He was a good hugger—never gave passive squeezes—but this time he held on a lot harder and longer than usual.

"How're you doing, Darling? Do you have questions?"

Tears showed again. "Is he saying I might have the same thing that killed Josh?"

"Yes, but Josh died a long time ago. Things have

changed. What Josh had can now be treated."

"Mom, I have never loved soccer as much as I do this very minute. If I have this heart thing, is there surgery so I can play again?"

"Yeah, I think there is."

"Okay, then if I have it, I want the surgery soon, so it won't mess up my season."

And for the first time that day, I started to cry, because here it was, that thing you can always count on embedded in adversity. Within minutes, Maliq's priorities had crystallized. He knew, without a doubt, what he was willing to do to keep the life he had previously taken for granted.

"Mom, is this going to be okay?"

I answered from the logical part of my brain. "It's going to be fine, and here's the good news; this morning, soccer got taken away, and when you get it back you'll appreciate it like you never have before."

"Mom, do you really believe that, or are you just being positive?"

This child knew me well. "I do believe it, and

I'm also being positive."

Finally at 9:45 that night, the cardiologist called. "The echo came back clean."

I let out the breath that I hadn't realized I'd been holding. "Great. That means Maliq doesn't have Marfan's or SADS?"

"You still need to meet with the geneticist, put all the pieces together."

The appointment with the geneticist ended up being scientifically interesting but thankfully, clinically insignificant. She found no Marfan's, and ruled out SADS.

Maliq started running sub-six-minute-miles. His soccer team made it to the state tournament and in a shoot-out where Maliq was up against arguably the best goalkeeper in the state, he blocked the most kicks and his team won.

Later, fork paused over the last of about ten meals he had eaten that day, he said, "Mom, I took it for granted before. I figured there was always time to get serious about soccer. Now, I know, I can't take anything for granted; we don't really ever know what kind of time we have."

I was so grateful that a lesson I learned through tragedy, this son was able to learn through a near miss.

—Lindsay A. Nielsen—

Unwrapping the Present

*A happy person is not a person in a certain
set of circumstances, but rather a person with
a certain set of attitudes.*
~Hugh Downs

I lay snugly in bed trying, yet again, to figure out what to do with my life. "God, what would you have me do? Where would you have me go?"

Too impatient to wait for His response, my mind catalogued everything I expected to hear: "Fight World Hunger." "Save the Children." "Stop Global Warming."

Yet I distinctly heard, "Go to Costco."

"Excuse me? Costco? Really?"

Not that I underestimate the spiritual value of seventy-five rolls of toilet paper, but maybe my to-do list got tangled up in my spiritual call. So I tried again.

"God, what would you have me do today? Where would you have me go?"

No doubt about it—"Costco" was His answer.

Frankly, I was relieved. Costco seemed infinitely more manageable than fighting world hunger, especially since I had to be home before 3:00 PM.

"If you have the nagging suspicion that you're wasting your life," Marianne Williamson, the spiritual teacher, once said, "it's because you are." Our house renovation, which had been my "job" for over a year, was finally finished and I now volunteered only minimally since my daughter had entered middle school. In short, I found myself suddenly out of work with that nagging suspicion Marianne talked about. Admittedly my ego yearned to own a cocktail-party sound bite that would impress when someone inevitably asked, "So what are you up to?"

"Uh... nothing."

In great need of an identity makeover, I'd begun reading spiritual books. What struck me was how often someone found her calling or purpose in life by waking each morning and asking God, "What would you have me do today? Where would you have me go?"

Truthfully it all seemed a little hooey. Could I really dial God 911 and get an answer?

But okay, I'd go with the flow. Maybe this Costco gig was my audition. If God saw that I could handle family hunger, he might give me a go at the world one day.

So I got out of bed and dressed for Costco.

Being Day One of my God-given duty, I approached my calling in, let's just say, a more godly way. Instead of weaving my shopping cart NASCAR-style through the aisles, running intersections, and whizzing through the less busy thoroughfares, I yielded. I turned off my cell phone and gave up being smug about multi-tasking, which I discovered enabled me to remember all of the items I came in for. But as I waited in the checkout line my foot tapped anxiously. I still had to go to the cleaners, the post office and the library and be home in thirty-five minutes. My heart raced faster. Breathe. Be here. Be present.

I redirected my thoughts to my feet and felt them ground me to the earth. As I breathed, tension evaporated. I became less stressed. I felt an opening of grace. I felt lighter.

I arrived home and unloaded my packed SUV. Normally, I'd moan about having to make multiple trips up two flights of stairs, including lugging a three-gallon jug of laundry detergent, but today I found gratitude. First, I was grateful I had the money to buy everything I did. Second, I was thankful my arms and legs were strong enough to haul my goods, and third, I was mindful we now had food for dinner and lunches and I could tackle the piles of laundry that had accumulated.

Gratitude was beginning to run rampant. The more present I became, the more I grasped how blessed I was. I was grateful I had appliances and that they worked. I was grateful every time I turned on the faucet and clean water came out. I was grateful I had a family to cook and clean for. Had my newly found gratitude not caused so much serenity, it could've been downright annoying.

"What's up with you?" my daughter asked, eyeing me suspiciously, as she dropped her book bag and kicked off her shoes. "You look weirdly happy."

I was happy. Not weirdly, just simply.

Being grateful—can that be a calling? My life's purpose?

My husband arrived home earlier than expected.

"Hi," I chirped.

His face was slack and drained of color, his eyes glazed with that "I have something to tell you but I don't want to" expression.

"My job's been 'downsized.' I haven't been fired, but I don't have a job."

I felt the panic of the unknown future surging through my body. What's going to happen? What now? What if? My body tightened. I felt ill.

Okay, gratitude's pretty easy when your pocket's full and the sun is shining, but I wasn't ready for this so soon. Now what, God? This was only my first day on the job.

Then it hit me. God didn't send me to Costco to find toilet paper, and the gratitude thing was really just a warm-up. What he sent me to find was presence.

I'd gotten it wrong. It wasn't God, what would you have me do? It was God, what would you have me be?

Be present. Be in this moment. Be.

I took a grounding breath and hugged my husband, absorbing the warmth of his body. As I stood in that present moment unwrapped, uncontested and accepted for simply what is, I understood that all we ever truly have is the present. Maintaining gratitude, faith and presence were actions I could choose now. Faith is knowing the moon is always full even if I see only a sliver or none at all. And from this deep place of awareness I knew we were, and would be, all right.

—Tsgoyna Tanzman—

The "Who Cares?" Bin

Only a few things are really important.
~Marie Dressler

I don't pray as much as I should. But two weeks ago I prayed as my husband, Bob, was taken by ambulance to Cape Cod Hospital with intensifying pain spreading through his chest.

There's exquisite simplicity and purity in the words "I love you" that two people share when it may be for the last time. And in that instant, everything else, every thought, every action, every other part of your life falls into the "who cares?" bin.

I want to tell you something very important. It is not a big deal to call 911. You call. They come. There'll be sirens, but you'll welcome their sound. The EMTs don't want you to wait until you're positive something's wrong.

Bob, on the couch, saw me struggling to quickly answer their questions through my crackly voice. And I wasn't breathing well. He mouthed the words, "I'm sorry," which, of course, broke my heart even more. Then he was taken away.

Ten minutes later, I hurried through the hospital parking lot with just one prayer. "Please let him be alive."

And my prayer was answered.

Joyously, I flopped down on the chair next to his gurney. Apparently, it wasn't his heart. We were bubbly with happiness.

The nurse connected leads from an EKG machine to different points on Bob's chest. As she unbuttoned his shirt, he looked at me and started to laugh. It was then I remembered his recent mid-life decision to try

Grecian Formula to get rid of the gray in his beard. But afraid to try it outright, he had experimented with his chest hair and was therefore sporting brown polka dots. The nurse was quiet. She also didn't say anything while Bob and I tried in vain to squelch a giggling fit.

"What have you eaten today?" she asked before taking blood.

"Jellybeans." By now, he had lost all credibility as a grown-up. After the EKG, he had X-rays. Then he was given a little plastic jar for a urinalysis. It took a heck of a long time for him to come out of the bathroom.

"What was the matter?" I asked when he came out. "Don't they have dirty magazines or something?"

"It wasn't that kind of test," he said, looking around in hopes I couldn't be heard.

So all continued well, until our drive home. Bob, feeling good, wanted to drive, but halfway down Main Street, I saw him reaching for his chest again.

"What is it?" I said, panicking.

He was feeling around. "They left these things on."

"What things?"

"They put BBs on my nipples so they wouldn't be mistaken for spots on my X-rays. But they're embedded in some sort of adhesive and I can't get them off."

I went ballistic. "You've got to get them off! What if we have an accident? What are people going to think if you're wearing nipple buttons?" I grabbed his nipples and started yanking. He swerved to park the car.

So, there I was, leaning over Bob's chest with my face in his nipples trying to wrench the BBs off. And a couple with three kids walked by, looked in the window, said something to each other, then ran away.

I'm learning to pray more. And one thing I've learned lately is to choose my prayers carefully. "Is this really important?" I'll ask myself, because if it's trivial or too selfish, I'll scrap it. And maybe prayer is really a process of evaluation that teaches me what matters and what doesn't.

And I'll tell you something else. Most of those things that fell into the "who cares?" bin during those terrible life and death moments… are going to stay right there.

Which is where, when it comes down to it, they should have been all along.

—Saralee Perel—

Childhood Delights

So our human life but dies down to its root,
and still puts forth its green blade to eternity.
~Henry David Thoreau

My mother was diagnosed with Alzheimer's long after I accepted the gradual changes I saw in her. I had grown used to partially listening to her repetitious stories and filling in the missing words of her sentences.

I imagine I might have continued to deny my inklings had she not been admitted to the hospital for a short hospital stay. During the night, apparently she had become disoriented and the nurses found her roaming the hallways. A neurology consultation had taken place and the doctor told me that my mother was approaching the middle stages of Alzheimer's.

The doctor was kind and compassionate as we sat in a hospital conference room. He explained that for people with dementia, once a memory was lost it could not be relearned as in the case of a stroke. I thought I understood that concept, but over the coming months, I often had to fight the urge to say, "I already told you that."

My mother lived with our family since her retirement. We enjoyed a deep friendship and she led a very independent life filled with activities. Almost overnight our family life dramatically changed with the pronouncement of that one word: Alzheimer's.

Those happy, active days dropped away from my consciousness as I suddenly felt trapped by the challenges that I imagined lay ahead for all of us. Somewhere in the process of hearing and accepting this diagnosis, my focus shifted from being with Mom to taking care of Mom.

Each day led to a new discovery as I learned what Mom knew and what she could no longer remember. For example, my heart sank the day I realized she could no longer read written directions. She stood in front of the microwave holding her frozen dinner, not knowing what do. That was also the day that I knew she would need someone to stay with her while I was at work. It was the only way I could ensure that she would eat during the day.

I thought about the best way to take care of Mom all the time. I was vigilant in my discreet observations of her. Looking back, I wonder if despite my well-meaning intentions, I arrogantly took it upon myself to decide what I thought was best. Possibly in the process I curbed some of her independence and neglected to consider her capability to express her feelings and opinions in the moment.

Driving the car was a major decision and dilemma as I wondered whether she could drive to the grocery store and find her way home. When was it time to remove her car keys from her purse? Fortunately it turned out to be a mutual agreement when she called me crying from the mall, "I can't find where I parked the car. Help me!" Thankfully she remembered the phone number, probably because she had dialed it hundreds of times over the years.

That one decision struck a major blow for each of us. It signaled a huge loss of independence for Mom and huge dependence on me. I also began wondering how I could convince her to wear a medical alert bracelet with her name and address without destroying her dignity.

Each day more memories were lost but slowly I discovered that every cloud does have a silver lining. Because my mother did not have memories of the past, I grew to know her in new and different ways that were free from the baggage that most of us carry throughout our lifetimes. Resentments with a sister-in-law no longer mattered and she would talk to her on the phone again. She could go to the hair salon on a Tuesday instead of a Saturday because each of her days really did begin with a clean slate.

Slowly I let go of the firm notion of taking care of Mom and being with Mom. We began to share a companionship. Often we would engage in an activity and it was as if she was experiencing it for the very first time. I would see delight on her face blowing out candles on her birthday cake, coloring with crayons, or picking flowers in the park.

It was surprising to see some amazing changes of imprinted patterns that evolved. She forgot that her back bothered her and I no longer had to drive around a parking lot to find the closest parking space to the store. She even began taking walks up and down our street.

One day we went to a buffet and I will admit I was a bit shocked and embarrassed when she stuck her hands in the salad bin and stacked her plate with a wide variety of foods. She didn't remember what she liked or disliked and I watched with fascination as she tried and enjoyed some of those foods.

As time passed, I noticed Mom was able to take care of herself in some new ways. She dressed herself but she didn't care if her clothes matched. This was the same person who bought me matching box-pleated skirts, cardigan sweaters, and knee socks as a child. I noticed with amusement and sadness that she took over the control of the television remote. Her taste in movies changed from her cherished classics to the Western channel.

She was unaware of the growing to-do list added to my schedule. She was free from paying bills, making dinner, driving herself to doctor appointments, laundry and numerous other details that make up a person's day.

Mostly she was happy just to be with me. She would follow me from room to room and was always ready to jump into the car for errands or an outing. Slowly I began to recognize her individuality as she displayed her likes and dislikes and a full range of unpredictable emotions. She was Mom, not just a human being with a disease.

One of my most treasured memories occurred when I took her to an outdoor band concert. They were playing music from the Big Band Era. By that time she was barely able to carry on a conversation, yet once the music started she sang the words to almost every song! For more than forty-five minutes, I was filled with awe and gratitude that somewhere deep inside her there was still a bridge to the outside world. I can still recall the joy and contentment on her face.

Alzheimer's helped me to learn to appreciate Mom and not just take care of her. As her memory fell away, I discovered in her an almost childlike innocence. She taught me to view the world from a different perspective and to notice how precious each moment can be. It is with a sense of irony that the less she remembered, the more present we both became in our lives.

—Jean Ferratier—

People First

*I always prefer to believe the best of
everybody, it saves so much trouble.*
~Rudyard Kipling

When I attended Open House at my son's school, I scanned the bulletin board outside his first-grade classroom. I spied Cody's handiwork in a colorful sea of papers tacked to the board. My expectant smile froze.

In one circle he was supposed to write or draw what he didn't like.

"MEN," he scrawled in capital letters.

Uh-oh, I thought as fear iced me. How could Cody not like men? He loved his daddy! Did some man do unspeakable things to my child?!

"Cody," I said casually. "Can you tell me about your work here?"

"Yeah," he replied, then carefully recited each word slowly. "I… don't… like… mean."

Such is the world of phonics, writing words the way they sound.

That exercise served to reinforce how our kids perceived the world, divided into two classes: good and bad.

It didn't matter to them what the person looked like. You were either good or you were bad. Take our neighbor next door, for instance. She was a good person, giving the kids treats when they deserved it. Now the bully on the bus who hit Cody in the stomach…

"He's mean, Mom!" cried Cody. "He's a bad boy!"

"He's not a bad boy," I replied, drying his tears. "What he DID was bad. There's a difference."

That's what the parenting magazines tell us to say. And it makes sense, this mass campaign of programming us to think in terms of "people coming first."

People with or without disabilities.

People with or without a steady income.

With or without a home.

With or without goodness.

People first.

But I doubted Cody understood my logic.

Until one warm Saturday morning.

Cody and I arrived at a pizza parlor where a birthday party was being held for his classmate, Kristi.

"Cody!" Kristi shouted, walking toward him in a cloud of pink ruffles, her thick, blond hair combed into one long braid down her back. She was radiant as she hugged him.

"Why, Kristi," I said, "you look beautiful!"

"Thank you," she responded, twirling around. "Let's go play some games, Cody!"

Cody, unfazed by being the only boy in the handful of attendees, bounced gleefully from one game to another, feeding tokens to hungry machines.

When several pizzas were delivered to the balloon-bedecked tables, Kristi made a point of asking Cody to sit next to her. When Cody asked for pink lemonade, she informed the waitress, with a trace of authority in her voice, "I'll have what he's having."

When it came time for opening presents, she announced, "I want to open Cody's present first!"

He handed her a small package, a pink Ooglie toy that made funny and irreverent noises when one pulled its tail.

"It's for your book bag," Cody said shyly.

"Oh, I love it!" she gushed, hugging Cody. "Thank you!"

While everyone was eating cake, Kristi leaned over to me and said, "Mrs. Oliver, Cody is always so nice to me every single day at school. He's the only one who's never, ever mean to me."

I blinked back tears. Not just because a little girl was sweet enough to acknowledge Cody's sensitivity to his mother. But for knowing how cruel kids could be, especially to skinny-challenged girls like Kristi.

My heart ached from the sudden surge of pride that coursed through it.

All I could think of was, by golly, he got it.

Cody got it.

People first.

—Jennifer Oliver—

Shiny Nickels

I don't think of all the misery but of the
beauty that still remains.
~Anne Frank

She had no business being so cheerful. All over the country people were out of work, losing homes, and being pushed into social services or the streets. Young people in the college classes I taught were cynical and apathetic. Why study hard when there'd be no jobs? Was I teaching skills and work ethics that might be meaningless? Was I encouraging false hope?

Yet each day in the front row forty-five-year-old Betty smiled eagerly. She was a big woman draped in shapeless sweatshirts and baggy jeans, her gray hair hung straight to her shoulders, and she shuffled with the painful effort of someone with arthritis. How could she compete in today's dog-eat-dog job market? If anyone should be sour, it was Betty. But her homework was always done thoroughly, and she waited for class to begin like a horse fidgeting at the starting gate.

It wasn't just that she earned straight A's, jumped into every discussion, and did extra research. She accepted no cynicism or apathy. One time we discussed a story about a man who freed a bird from a zoo hunter's live trap so it could rejoin its mate that hovered in the sky overhead. Betty sighed, "I'm glad somebody does things like that. It's beautiful!"

A young man scoffed. "What's one bird more or less? It would've lived longer in captivity. Besides, they'll just catch another one. Do you know how much money people make capturing rare birds?"

Betty smiled. "That's true. But what counts is the moment when the birds meet again in the sky.

Picture that and forget the rest. It doesn't matter if hunters catch another one, if the birds die, or if the world explodes. You have to live for those shining moments or why live? Life is full of loss and death. That's not news. You young people think the world is falling apart, but it's not. I know what real disaster is. My husband died last year. My daughter has kidney disease. We have no health insurance or income." The young man's face reddened. Betty smiled. "No, don't feel bad. How could you know? It's all right. Just because bad stuff happens doesn't make life bad. It should teach us to love what's good now. Don't wait for money and success to light up your life. You've got to grab the little shiny moments that come to all of us while they're here."

Yes, I thought. That's what I ought to be telling my students—and myself.

A week later I saw someone bending deep into a trash bin in the student union. It was common these days for homeless men to comb the college trash for beverage cans redeemable for five cents each. But when this person straightened up with two cans, it was Betty. I hesitated to greet her. Being caught raiding the trash by her professor might be embarrassing. Heck, it embarrassed me. As I tried to slip by, she noticed me, and her face brightened. "Professor!"

"Hello."

"I collect cans between classes. It's my bus fare! It's amazing what people throw away, even in times like this." She dropped the cans into a bag. "Actually, it's wonderful. I come to college each day with an empty purse. Not a cent sometimes! But I always find enough cans for bus fare and sometimes lunch too. They're waiting for me every day."

"Suppose you can't find enough?"

She laughed and shrugged. "I could hike home if I had to, I guess. But they just keep coming. What a person needs is usually there if you search hard." I told her that if she ever fell short, to stop by my office. She smiled. "See? Now I have bus fare insurance!"

I drew her aside from the streaming crowd. "You know, what you said in class last week really hit those young people hard. They've been writing about it. You made them see things differently. Me too," I admitted.

"I'm glad. Maybe even suffering can do some good."

"I'm so sorry about your husband."

"Oh, I won't lie. For a long time I was broken without him. Broken in pieces. And it's been horrible trying to survive. He died two months before qualifying for his pension and of course the health insurance expired when we needed it most. I'm lucky I still have him to hang onto."

"What do you mean?"

She smiled. "I love him so much, just like always. Every night I think about how we'd lie in bed and read and talk, sometimes until 3 AM. We owned a rickety old house, but we had dreams. Oh, such shiny dreams! You can't ever take that away from a person who wants to hold onto it. I'm alone in an apartment now, but we're still in love and married. It's just that he's dead. We'll meet again someday, just like the birds in the story."

"What will you do about your daughter?"

"The doctor says her kidneys might last another five years. I'd give her one of mine, but we don't match. We'll just have to see what happens. I can't control what fate brings. I can only control how I respond to it. So why choose misery? Isn't it wonderful enough just to have lived? To have felt and seen and tasted life? Bill and I made sure our daughter did that. She won't die without having lived."

I suggested several agencies that might help with her daughter's medical bills. "Oh, I know them," she said. "We're working on that. And here I am at my age starting college to get a decent job!" She laughed. "Bill would love that! Those young people don't think jobs are out there. But you can find one if you look hard and aren't afraid to get dirty. There's a job out there that I'll find." She shook her bag so the cans rattled. "These aren't garbage. They're not recyclable aluminum. They're shiny nickels."

—Garrett Bauman—

Meet Our Contributors

Garrett Bauman has recently retired as a professor of English at Monroe Community College in Rochester, NY and is the author of a book on writing, *Ideas and Details*, 7th edition published by Cengage. He plays tennis, kayaks, gardens and writes about his students and family. He can be contacted via e-mail at mbauman@monroecc.edu.

Elaine L. Bridge worked in the woods on the West Coast as a forester before becoming a stay-at-home mom to her three boys. Now living in Ohio she works part-time in a grocery store and is devoted to developing her relationship with God, caring for her family and writing inspirational material.

Jean Ferratier holds a degree in Psychology and a Masters in Early Childhood Education. Her passion is learning and sharing information through inspirational stories for children and adults. She enjoys teaching and spiritual mentoring. Dancing and participating in the arts are her special interests. Please contact her via e-mail at jferratier@gmail.com.

Kids, critters, and country music give **Annie Mannix** plenty of raw material to inspire her tales about the sparks and giggles of everyday life. More of her stories can be found at www.anniesway.blogspot.com, and you can contact her via e-mail at eitman@mindspring.com.

Lindsay Nielsen is an author, psychotherapist, public speaker and athlete (2000 Paralympics) and was the first female amputee to complete an Ironman Triathlon. Lindsay is completing a memoir; *If You're Not Dead, It's Not Too Late! An amputee's triumphant run through love, loss and world records*. Please visit her website; www.lindsaynielsen.com.

Hailing from Copperas Cove, TX, **Jennifer Oliver** owes her inspiration to househubby, Stephen, and to their magnificent creative life forces: Cody, Ethan, Matthew, and Madison. Her stories have appeared in several *Chicken Soup for the Soul* books and other heartwarming publications.

Saralee Perel is an award-winning columnist/novelist and multiple contributor to *Chicken Soup for the Soul*. Her book, *The Dog Who Walked Me*, is about her dog who became her caregiver after Saralee's spinal cord injury, the initial devastation of her marriage, and her cat who kept her sane. Contact her at sperel saraleeperel.com or www.saraleeperel.com.

Tom Schumm is an inspirational speaker who received a BA from Alma College, and an MBA from the University of Michigan. He enjoys boating, travel, opera, and collecting antique fruit jars. He is currently writing a book about his journey with brain cancer. Please e-mail him at tomschumm.pma@gmail.com.

Diane Stark is a wife, mother, teacher, and writer. Her work has been printed in dozens of publications. She writes about the important things in life: her family and her faith. She is the author of *Teachers' Devotions to Go* and she can be reached via e-mail at DianeStark19@yahoo.com.

Writer, speech therapist, memoir teacher, wife and mother, **Tsgoyna Tanzman** credits writing as the supreme "therapy" for raising an adolescent daughter. Published in numerous *Chicken Soup for the Soul* books, her humorous essays and poems can be read on More.com, motheringmagazine.com, and in *The Orange County Register*. E-mail her at tnzmn@cox.net.

Meet
Amy Newmark

Amy Newmark is the bestselling author, editor-in-chief, and publisher of the *Chicken Soup for the Soul* book series. Since 2008, she has published 150 new books, most of them national bestsellers in the U.S. and Canada, more than doubling the number of Chicken Soup for the Soul titles in print today. She is also the author of *Simply Happy*, a crash course in Chicken Soup for the Soul advice and wisdom that is filled with easy-to-implement, practical tips for having a better life.

Amy is credited with revitalizing the Chicken Soup for the Soul brand, which has been a publishing industry phenomenon since the first book came out in 1993. By compiling inspirational and aspirational true stories curated from ordinary people who have had extraordinary experiences, Amy has kept the twenty-four-year-old Chicken Soup for the Soul brand fresh and relevant.

Amy graduated *magna cum laude* from Harvard University where she majored in Portuguese and minored in French. She then embarked on a three-decade career as a Wall Street analyst, a hedge fund manager, and a corporate executive in the technology field. She is a Chartered Financial Analyst.

Her return to literary pursuits was inevitable, as her honors thesis in college involved traveling throughout Brazil's impoverished northeast region, collecting stories from regular people. She is delighted to have come full circle in her writing career — from collecting stories "from the people" in Brazil as a twenty-year-old to, three decades later, collecting stories "from the people" for Chicken Soup for the Soul.

When Amy and her husband Bill, the CEO of Chicken Soup for the Soul, are not working, they are visiting their four grown children and their first grandchild.

Follow Amy on Twitter @amynewmark. Listen to her free podcast — "Chicken Soup for the Soul with Amy Newmark" — on Apple Podcasts, Google Play, the Podcasts app on iPhone, or by using your favorite podcast app on other devices.

Changing lives one story at a time®
www.chickensoup.com